D1159725

The Countries

China

Bob Italia

ABDO Publishing Company

visit us at
www.abdopub.com

Published by ABDO Publishing Company, 4940 Viking Drive, Edina, Minnesota 55435.
Copyright © 2001 by Abdo Consulting Group, Inc. International copyrights reserved in
all countries. No part of this book may be reproduced in any form without written
permission from the publisher.

Printed in the United States.

Photos: Corbis
Editors: Tamara L. Britton, Kate A. Furlong, and Christine Fournier
Art Direction & Maps: Neil Klinepier

Library of Congress Cataloging-in-Publication Data

Italia, Bob, 1955-
    China / Bob Italia.
        p. cm. -- (Countries)
    Includes index.
    ISBN 1-57765-492-7
    1. China--Juvenile literature. [1. China] I. Title. II. Series.

    DS706 .I87 2001
    951--dc21

                                                    2001016127

Contents

Ni Hao!

Hello from China! China is a huge country. More than 1 billion people live there! They have established a **culture** unlike any other in the world.

China is home to one of the world's oldest civilizations. Its cities are filled with historic buildings and art. Its lands are full of natural wonders.

Today, China opens the door to the whole world. With a booming **economy**, the ancient country is becoming more modern. People from all over the world are exploring China.

Ni Hao *from China!*

Fast Facts

OFFICIAL NAME: People's Republic of China

CAPITAL: Beijing

LAND
- Highest Mountain Range: Himalayas
- Highest Point: Mount Everest 29,000 feet (8,850 m)
- Lowest Point: Turpan Pendi -505 feet (-154 m)
- Major River: Yangtze

PEOPLE
- Population: 1.3 billion (2000 est.)
- Major Cities: Shanghai, Beijing, Hong Kong
- Language: Chinese (Mandarin)
- Religion: Officially atheist; Buddism, Confucianism, Taoism, Islam, and Christianity also practiced

GOVERNMENT
- Form: Communist state
- Head of Government: Premier
- Head of State: President
- Legislature: National People's Congress
- Flag: Red with a large yellow star and four smaller stars
- Nationhood: 1949 (People's Republic of China formed)

ECONOMY
- Agricultural Products: Rice, wheat, potatoes, sorghum, peanuts, tea, millet, barley, cotton, oilseed, pork, fish
- Mining Products: Coal, iron ore, petroleum
- Manufactured Products: Cement, petroleum products, steel, cotton, silk, textiles, vegetable oils, raw sugar, fertilizers, plastics, machines
- Money: Yuan

BEIJING

China's Flag

Yuan

Timeline

1766 B.C.	China's first dynasty begins
A.D. 105	Paper invented
600s	Porcelain invented
700s	Printing invented
900s	Gunpowder invented
1100s	Compass invented
1500s	Europeans begin trading with the Chinese
1900	Boxer Rebellion forces foreigners out of China
1911	China's last dynasty ends; a new republic forms
1949	A communist government overtakes China
1989	Students protest at Tiananmen Square
1997	England returns Hong Kong to China

China's Past

China has been a center of civilization for thousands of years. Its people have shared a common **culture** longer than any other group in the world.

Dynasties ruled China for much of its history. The first dynasty was the Shang Dynasty. It began in about 1766 B.C. Different dynasties ruled China for about the next 3,000 years.

During the rule of the dynasties, China's people created an advanced civilization. They invented paper, printing, gunpowder, porcelain, and the compass.

In the 1500s, trading ships from Europe began coming to China. European merchants traded wool and spices for Chinese tea, silk, **opium**, and porcelain.

Slowly, Europeans gained more power in China. This led to the Boxer Rebellion in 1900. It was a movement to make foreigners leave China. Many people died.

Chinese merchants meet along the banks of a river.

China's last **dynasty** ended in 1911. That year, a man named Sun Yat-sen (suhn YAHT-sen) started a republican government in China. But slowly, **communists** gained power. In 1949, they overtook China's government and formed the People's Republic of China.

A man named Mao Zedong (mao zeh-dung) led the new government. He ruled China for nearly 30 years. During this time, he created many plans to make China more modern. His plans tried to improve China's **economy** and living conditions.

Some Chinese people thought the government mistreated its citizens. So in 1989, a group of students met in Tiananmen Square to protest. The government killed hundreds of the protesters.

Today, the communist government still rules China. It has developed China into a more modern nation. The nation's power seems greater than ever as it plays an important role in world affairs.

Chairman Mao Zedong

A Vast Land

China is in Asia. It is the third-largest country in the world. Only Russia and Canada are larger. China's vast land includes mountains, plains, rivers, deserts, and islands.

Along the east, China borders the Pacific Ocean. About 5,000 islands lay along China's coastline. The two largest islands are Taiwan (TY-WAHN) and Hainan (HY-NAHN).

Mountains cover much of China's land. They stretch across western China and gradually slope down into plains in the east. The Himalayas are an important mountain range in China. They contain Mount Everest, which borders China and Nepal. Mount Everest is the world's highest point.

China also has deserts. The Taklimakan (tah-kluh-muh-KHAN) Desert lies in northwestern China. It is the country's largest desert. It is one of the most barren places in the world.

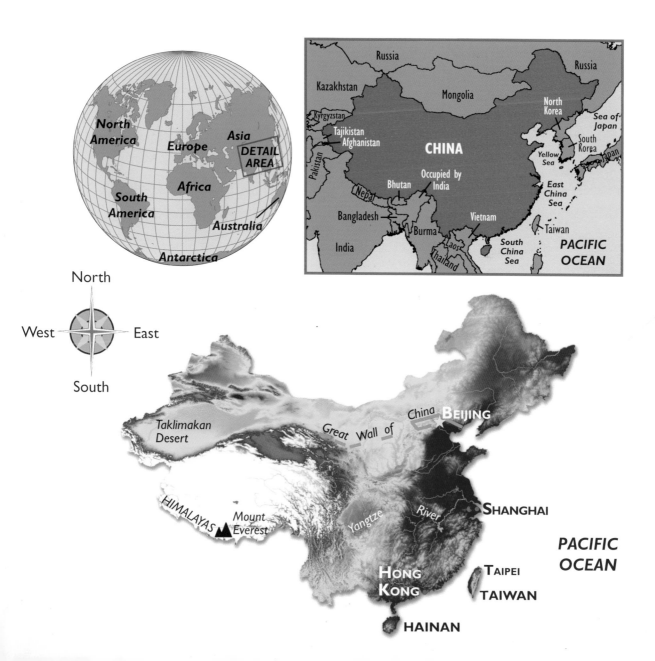

North America
Europe
Asia
DETAIL AREA
Africa
South America
Australia
Antarctica

Russia
Kazakhstan
Mongolia
Russia
Kyrgyzstan
Tajikistan
Afghanistan
North Korea
Sea of Japan
South Korea
Japan
Pakistan
CHINA
Yellow Sea
Nepal
Bhutan
Occupied by India
East China Sea
Bangladesh
Burma
Vietnam
India
Laos
Thailand
Taiwan
South China Sea
PACIFIC OCEAN

North
West   East
South

Taklimakan Desert
Great Wall of China
BEIJING
HIMALAYAS
Mount Everest
Yangtze
River
SHANGHAI
PACIFIC OCEAN
HONG KONG
TAIPEI
TAIWAN
HAINAN

China has many rivers. The Yangtze (YANG-see) flows across central China. It is the country's longest river.

Climates vary greatly in China. Northern China has cold winters and warm summers. Central and southern China have short, cold winters and long, hot summers.

China's rainy season lasts from April to September. During this time, monsoons can hit the southeast coast. These storms bring heavy rains and wind.

The Yangtze River flows across China for 3,900 miles (6,300 km).

Rainfall

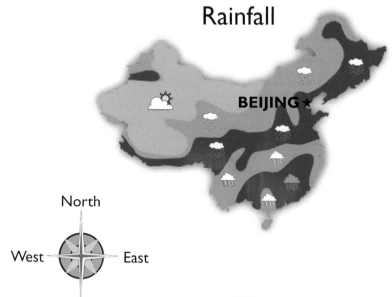

BEIJING ★

North

West — East

South

AVERAGE YEARLY RAINFALL

Inches		Centimeters
Under 10		Under 25
10 - 20		25 - 50
20 - 40		50 - 100
40 - 60		100 - 150
60 - 80		150 - 200

Temperature

AVERAGE TEMPERATURE

Fahrenheit		Celsius
68° - 86°		20° - 30°
50° - 68°		10° - 20°
32° - 50°		0° - 10°
14° - 32°		-10° - 0°
-4° - 14°		-20° - -10°
-22° - -4°		-30° - -20°
Under -22°		Under -30°

Winter

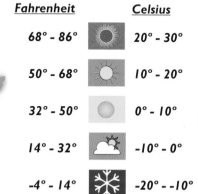

BEIJING ★

Summer

BEIJING ★

Plants & Animals

China's vast land is home to many kinds of plants. But much of China's plant life is suffering. Farmers have cut down many trees to make grazing land and fields.

Despite these problems, many plants still grow in China. Tropical forests grow in the south. Pine forests cover the north. Grasslands border China's deserts. **Mangrove** swamps grow along the coast.

One of China's best-known plants is bamboo. It is a tall, treelike grass that grows in the tropical forests. Bamboo has many uses. It can be eaten, prepared as medicine, or used to build houses and bridges.

China has many flowering plants, too. One is called the lotus. It grows in the water. It has large, round leaves and yellow or pink flowers.

Lotus flowers

A bamboo forest

China has many kinds of wildlife, too. Some of these animals include monkeys, alligators, rabbits, yaks, tigers, leopards, deer, camels, elephants, cranes, ducks, and swans. These animals live in China's forested hills or in its lakes and rivers.

One of China's most famous animals is the giant panda. Pandas live in China's mountains and forests. They do not live anyplace else on earth. Pandas are in danger of becoming **extinct**. China's government is working to protect these rare creatures.

Though China has a wide variety of animals, many are in danger. Humans have begun to move into areas that animals need to survive. Farms, cities, and pollution have destroyed the **habitats** of many animals in China.

Opposite page: A giant panda plays in a tree at the Wolong Natural Reserve in Sichuan, China.

China's People

China has many different groups of people. The majority of China's people belong to the Han group. Han people have been in China for thousands of years. They share the same **culture** and language. More than 55 minority groups also live in China.

China's official language is Chinese. Chinese has many different **dialects**. The official dialect is Mandarin. It is the dialect most Chinese people speak. Cantonese is another widely-spoken Chinese dialect.

The Chinese language is written using symbols called characters. Each character represents a word or idea. In elementary school, Chinese children learn nearly 3,000 different characters.

Elementary schools are available to nearly all of China's children. Children begin school when they are about seven years old. They learn reading, math, music, art, and science. Students can then go to middle school and high school.

The art of writing characters is called calligraphy.

Religion in China has changed since the **communist** government took over in 1949. The government thought religion weakened the country. So it made China **atheist.** Then it closed many of China's temples and churches.

Today, a few of the temples and churches have reopened. There, people practice Buddhism, Confucianism (kuhn-FEW-shuhn-izuhm), and Taoism (DOW-izuhm). Some Chinese people also practice Islam or Christianity.

A majority of Chinese people live in the countryside. They live on farms and in villages. Village houses are built close together. They are made of sun-dried brick or pounded earth. Footpaths often connect nearby villages.

In China's cities, many people live in tall apartment buildings. They are usually made of brick or concrete. In many apartments, families share public kitchens and bathrooms.

A village in rural China

People in China wear many types of clothing. Traditional clothing includes long robes, loose pants, and **tunics**. Many people also wear modern clothes such as blue jeans, sweaters, skirts, and business suits.

China's people eat a wide variety of foods. People like to eat duck, chicken, fish, and fresh fruits and vegetables. Steamed bread, rice, and noodles are also popular. Tea is the most common drink in China. But American soft drinks are becoming popular, too.

In China, people eat their food with chopsticks.

Noodles & Peanut Sauce

2 tbsp creamy peanut butter
3 tbsp soy sauce
4 cups cooked spaghetti noodles

1/4 cup hot water
1 tsp honey
1/2 cup peanuts, chopped

In a bowl, mix peanut butter and water until creamy, then add the soy sauce and honey. Add the cooked spaghetti noodles to the bowl with the peanut butter sauce. Toss well, top with chopped peanuts, and serve.

AN IMPORTANT NOTE TO THE CHEF: Always have an adult help with the preparation and cooking of food. Never use kitchen utensils or appliances without adult permission and supervision.

People with peanut allergies should not eat this dish.

English	Chinese (Mandarin)
Yes	Shi de
No	Bu
Thank You	Xiexie
Please	Qing
Hello	Ni Hao
Goodbye	Zaijian
Mother	Muqin
Father	Fuqin

LANGUAGE

Earning a Living

Farming is an important part of China's **economy**. Many people work as farmers. They grow rice, wheat, sweet potatoes, tobacco, and cotton. Farmers also raise livestock, such as chickens and pigs.

China's land is rich in minerals. So mining is another valuable part of its economy. People mine coal, **petroleum**, and iron. These minerals can be sold to other countries or manufactured into finished goods.

Manufacturing is a growing part of China's economy. Factory workers make cement, petroleum products, steel, and **textiles**. They also make electronic goods, such as television sets and radios.

Much of the energy that powers China's factories and cities comes from minerals. Coal and oil are China's main energy sources. Some energy also comes from the country's many waterways.

Chinese farmers harvest rice.

Cities & Regions

China has the world's largest population. More than 1 billion people live there. Millions of these people live in China's cities.

Shanghai (shang-HY) is China's largest city. More than 7 million people live there. The city is located near the Yangtze River and the East China Sea. This makes Shanghai an important trading city.

Beijing (BAY-JING) is the capital of China. It is home to a famous area called the Forbidden City. For more than 500 years, it was home to China's **dynasties**. Today, visitors can see some of China's oldest buildings there.

Hong Kong is a region in China. It covers 234 islands and part of the mainland. For 150 years, England controlled Hong Kong. Then in 1997, England returned it to China. Today, Hong Kong continues to attract tourists and traders alike.

The island of Taiwan is another important part of China. Its capital city is Taipei. For many years, China and Taiwan have struggled for control of the island.

Downtown Shanghai

Moving About

The Chinese use many methods to travel in their large country. China has many modern airports. China's airlines fly to cities within China. They also fly to neighboring countries, Europe, Africa, and the U.S.

Trains are another important kind of transportation. China has 32,000 miles (52,000 km) of railway. Trains transport people and goods through the country.

In the cities, people often ride buses. Long-distance buses carry people across China's countryside. People also drive cars and motorcycles.

Many Chinese people ride bicycles to get around. More than 300 million bicycles can be found in China. They are often sturdy and can carry a rider plus a large load.

China also uses boats for transportation. **Ferries** carry people between cities along the coast. Ships travel through China's deep rivers and harbors.

Bicyclists in China

Ruling China

China is a **communist** country. That means the Communist Party controls the government. Party members hold China's most important government jobs.

China's people can vote once they turn 18. They elect people to local congresses. In turn, the local congresses elect people to the National People's Congress (NPC).

The NPC is China's most powerful government body. Three thousand members serve on the NPC. They make laws and elect China's president and premier.

The president and premier are China's two main leaders. The president is the head of state. His job is mostly ceremonial. The premier is the head of government. He leads the State Council. It controls China's defense, **economy**, education, and **culture**.

Two parts of China have different governments. Hong Kong's government is called a Special Administrative

Region. Taiwan's government is called the Republic of China. Both Hong Kong and Taiwan have their own leaders and lawmaking groups.

An opening session of the National People's Congress

Celebrations

The Chinese New Year starts on the first day of the **Chinese calendar**, which is usually in February. People feast, visit relatives, and attend parades. They hope their celebrations will bring luck, health, happiness, and wealth to the new year.

The Chinese New Year lasts 15 days. Then the Lantern Festival takes place. It marks the end of the New Year celebrations. On this day, people make or buy paper lanterns. At night, they walk around the streets carrying them.

China has many other holidays, too. On Tomb Sweep Day, people clean the tombs of their ancestors. During the Dragon Boat Festival, people gather to watch dragon boat races. During the Moon Festival, people light firecrackers, gaze at the moon, and eat moon cakes.

A boy carries lanterns to celebrate the Lantern Festival.

Experiencing China

People in China can take part in many different outdoor activities. Bicycle tours are popular **pastimes**. In the deserts, people can take camel rides. Some people like to ice-skate and ski in the winter.

Many people enjoy attending China's theaters. Chinese theater is often called opera because it contains so much music. Traditional Chinese music uses instruments such as flutes, banjos, fiddles, and gongs.

China's beautiful art is famous throughout the world. Chinese paintings are often of landscapes. The paintings are made in black ink on fine paper or silk.

One of the country's most famous attractions is the Great Wall of China. People began building the wall about 2,000 years ago to protect China's empire. Today, it stands as one of the largest construction projects ever carried out by humans.

The Great Wall of China is 1,500 miles (2,400 km) long.

Glossary

atheist - a person or group that does not believe in God.

Chinese calendar - a calendar based on the phases of the moon.

communism - a social and economic system in which everything is owned by the government and given to the people as needed.

culture - the customs, arts, and tools of a nation or people at a certain time.

dialect - a form of language that is spoken in a particular area or by a particular group. Some of its grammar and vocabulary may differ from other forms of the same language.

dynasty - a series of rulers who belong to the same family.

economy - the way a nation uses its money, goods, and natural resources.

extinct - something that no longer exists.

ferry - a boat that carries people and goods across a body of water.

habitat - a place where a living thing is naturally found.

mangrove - trees or shrubs that have many above-ground roots. They often grow in tropical areas.

opium - a drug made from the poppy plant.

pastime - something that amuses and makes time pass pleasantly.

petroleum - a thick, yellowish-black oil. It is the source of gasoline.

textiles - of or having to do with the designing, manufacturing, or producing of woven fabric.

tunic - a piece of clothing that looks like a long shirt. It may reach to the knee or below.

Web Sites

Beijing, China
http://www.beijing.gov.cn/english/index.htm
Learn more about China's capital city on this site, sponsored by Beijing's government.

Chinese Holidays
http://www.gio.gov.tw/info/festival_c/index_e.htm
This kid-friendly site sponsored by Taiwan's government has information on traditional Chinese holidays.

Walk the Wall
http://www.peterdanford.com/greatwall/
This site allows visitors to take a virtual tour of the Great Wall of China.

These sites are subject to change. Go to your favorite search engine and type in "China" for more sites.

Index